Storage

Tessa Shaw started her career working as a news and fashion reporter on photographer David Bailey's fashion magazine, *Fashion Weekly*. Since 1982, she has been producing, presenting and reporting for television and radio. She has presented the BBC *Home Front* series since 1995. Tessa has two sons and not enough storage space in her North London home.

home front
Storage

TESSA SHAW

BBC Books

To my father,
who would have been more than a little amused to see me
connected in any way with tidiness.

Photographs: Mark Gatehouse
Illustrations: Claire Davies

This book is published to accompany the
BBC Television series *Home Front*.

Series Producer: Mary Sackville-West
Editor: Daisy Goodwin

Published by BBC Books, an imprint of
BBC Worldwide Ltd., Woodlands, 80 Wood Lane,
London, W12 0TT

First published 1998

ISBN 0 563 38388 7

Commissioning Editor: Nicky Copeland
Project Editor: Judy Spours
In-house Editor: Jane Parsons
Designer: Jane Parry
Stylist: Kay McGlone

Set in Futura
Printed and bound in France by Imprimerie Pollina s.a.
Colour separations by Imprimerie Pollina s.a.
Cover printed by Imprimerie Pollina s.a.

Contents

Foreword   6
Introduction   7

CLOTHES AND SHOES   12

Built-in systems   14
Floor to ceiling   16
Recessed cupboard   19
Curtained wardrobe   20
Dressed up   21
Children's clothes   24

COLLECTABLES AND CLUTTER   26

Clutter solutions   29
Recycled wooden shelf   33
Stairwells and hallways   34
Books and magazines   36
Sound systems   37
Album shelving   38

OFFICE STUDIES   40

Working from home   42
Spare room study   46
Working life   48
Cube shelving   49
Versatile desks   50

FOOD AND DRINK FILE   52

Small kitchen spaces   54
Visibly clean lines   56
Kitchen pan rail   58
Rustic recycling   60
Free-standing pantry   63
Fabric-lined doors   65

BATHROOMS AND LAUNDRY   66

Laundry   68
Ship-shape pulley system   70
Hanging glass shelves   75

ROOM FOR THE CHILDREN   76

Crafts cupboard   78
High-rise living   81
Castle toy cupboard   82

BASEMENTS AND SHEDS   84

Hang up that clobber   86
The garden shed   90

Sources   94
Acknowledgements   95
Index   96

Foreword

Whatever you think about storage, we all need it. This book contains my ideas about how you can have a go at storing your things without needing a complete personality change. I'm not a storage guru, I'm not a tidy person, but even I can see the benefits of knowing where my keys are when I rush out in the morning. This book is an attempt to suggest lots of easy, practical and inexpensive ways of *sorting out your stuff*.

We've all got different tastes, thankfully, so what you store your things in depends on you, but what I'm trying to get to the bottom of is how we go about that storing. How do we get to those decisions to alphebetize our books or colour code our clothes? I still have those horrible cupboards that I plan to clear out one day, just like everyone else, but I have managed to think differently about most of the space I use daily. It now pretty much works, given the occasional blitz when things get out of hand. And that certainly wasn't true a few years ago. It might have something to do with meeting and living with someone much tidier than me, which made me realize that getting your storage sorted benefits your relationships as much as your state of mind.

RIGHT: STORAGE IS AN AGE-OLD PROBLEM. HERE ARE MEDIEVAL SHELVES AND CUPBOARDS IN AN ILLUSTRATION FROM A FRENCH TRANSLATION OF ARISTOTLE'S *ETHICS, POLITICS, ECONOMICS*.

Introduction

Storage is not a new subject – it has been going on for ever. While we might use brightly coloured boxes to store our things in now, people have been storing their possessions ever since they possessed any! The same old principles apply now as then. We store to protect and preserve our things. Sometimes we want to hide them away and sometimes we want to display them. How we do that depends on our sense of style and our energy and, of course, our attitude to clutter.

As shops have caught up with our desires to have more colourful items around us, it is now no longer difficult to find great, inexpensive ideas for storing everything from CDs to documents. Only a couple of years ago, for example, no one thought office furniture should look exciting, even though many of us were forced to have it at home. It's probably part of the reason for a revival in interest in 1950s desks and office fittings and a greater availability of new and retro products designed solely for storage. Poking around in junk shops and salvage yards can still uncover lovely old cupboards and bits of wood which make great storage.

Storage is about things and what to do with them, so it seems logical to organize this book by objects rather than by rooms. Most of our rooms double-up as something else – the office as a spare room, the children's bedroom as playroom – so storage has to be adaptable to many and varied themes. With flexibility in mind, this book gives you ideas that will work whatever your situation and however much space you have.

Dealing with your clutter is as much about deciding what to do as it is about actually doing it. As long as you decide on a system and stick to it, it will work. So, whether you sort your books alphabetically or by subject, or even by size, if you can find them, it works.

Once you have decided to get organized, sit down, have a cup

ABOVE: YOU CAN TELL HE'S AN ART DIRECTOR: EVERYTHING IS ARRANGED NEATLY WITH EVERY BIT OF SPACE USED WISELY.

RIGHT: OLD AND NEW FIT TOGETHER WITHOUT CONFLICT IN A HOME OFFICE.

of tea and work out what you want from your rooms. Don't attempt too much at one go. Take one room and think about what you use it for, what you need to store in it and where it fails. It is far better to finish one than to have all your rooms in a state of chaos. You just get overwhelmed and give up.

It is important to consider your budget and to decide whether you want permanent or temporary storage. It may be that you want to go for built-in cupboards, or you may prefer free-standing furniture which you can take with you when you move. You may find that simple carpentry which you've

designed ends up cheaper and is far more original than ready-made items bought from the shops. Decide on the look you want. and think carefully about whether you will be able to maintain the look. There is no point in having open shelving with neatly folded T-shirts the first week, which degenerates into a dilapidated pile the next.

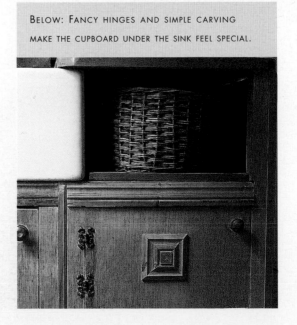

BELOW: FANCY HINGES AND SIMPLE CARVING MAKE THE CUPBOARD UNDER THE SINK FEEL SPECIAL.

LEFT: BE CREATIVE AND BUILD YOUR OWN STYLISH DRESSER WITH RECYCLED WOOD AND DECORATIVE SPINDLES.

RIGHT: IT'S WORTH MAKING THE MOST OF THE SPACE UNDERNEATH THE BED. IF THE BOXES FIT WELL, YOU WILL AVOID DUST SETTLING.

ABOVE: OH, TO HAVE THIS MANY
CLOTHES! IF THEY LOOK THIS GOOD,
DISPLAY THEM. EVERY BIT OF SPACE
RIGHT UP TO THE CEILING IS USED.

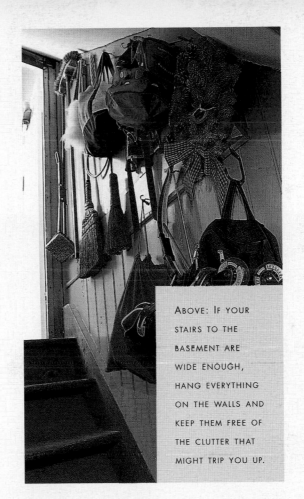

ABOVE: IF YOUR
STAIRS TO THE
BASEMENT ARE
WIDE ENOUGH,
HANG EVERYTHING
ON THE WALLS AND
KEEP THEM FREE OF
THE CLUTTER THAT
MIGHT TRIP YOU UP.

STARTING THE WORK

Once you get started, the most obvious and yet most often ignored tip is to throw away what you don't need. Look at your stuff and decide if you will ever use an item again. If not, get rid of it. If you want to keep it, think how often you will use it and then store it in the right place.

When you single out storage, it immediately becomes clear that it is as important as working out where the furniture is to go. If you get it right, everyone in your home will thank you for it. And you will find that there's more time to do what you thought you never had time for!

Clothes and *Shoes*

Clothes and shoes are often big investments and if looked after will serve you well. How you store them shows how you value them. You may get pleasure from displaying your jumpers or want to hide everything away and preserve it from the moths. Whatever your style, clothes and shoes are one area where you have to make decisions. Everyone wears them!

Built-in Systems

Not many people are lucky enough to be able to devote a whole area to storing their clothes and shoes, not to mention having such beautiful clothes to display. If you have the space and clothes, it must be the ultimate luxury to organize your wardrobe like this. For me, this is my dream storage space: it's totally organized without being uptight and stuffy. The clothes breathe and you can enjoy their fabrics and colours, yet there's plenty of room to hide away all the items you don't want to see every day.

Generous and sophisticated storage space can easily be achieved even if you don't have a whole room to devote to it. Using simple carpentry, you can create a whole wall of cupboard space, designing the drawers and hanging space to suit your needs. Often, starting from scratch can be the best option as you're not trying to build around other people's existing designs.

Think what sort of person you are. Do you have time to rearrange your jumpers neatly and will you fold your T-shirts and stack them carefully in your display shelving? Will it give you pleasure when you've done it? I like the idea of being tidy, but I know that it's handy to have cupboards to hide things in, too. Use the whole wall. Too often people build shelving to suit their height and end up with dead space at the top of a room. It's useful to have high-level cupboards

ABOVE: DRESSING MADE EASY – THE CLOTHES ARE GROUPED BY COLOUR AND THE HANGERS ALL FACE NEATLY TO THE BACK OF THE CUPBOARD.

for things you don't need much or which you don't want people to find!

In our picture, the couple have exciting, colourful clothes fit to be displayed. If your clothes are mainly black you may not want to show them off. If you have small children with sticky fingers, doors are a definite plus.

Don't forget the person or people you live with. Will they co-operate, and is your design simple enough to make life easier for them? If it isn't, you will get furious as you try in vain to impose your own structure.

BELOW: A PURPOSE-BUILT, WALK-IN DRESSING ROOM BETWEEN THE BATHROOM AND BEDROOM, DESIGNED FOR MINIMUM TIME WASTING. YOU CAN TELL THAT THE OWNERS OF THESE CUPBOARDS HAVE THEIR LIVES SORTED!

Floor to Ceiling

I feel I know this room. I've lived in so many like it, and used the space equally badly. Everything is crammed on a horrible mantelpiece just because it's there and the alcove ends up with a clothes rail as it's quick and easy to do. And the effect is a mess.

This room is a classic example of the way most of us live. We never take the time to look at the rooms we spend so much time in. The owner hated the louvred doors covering the fireplace, which had been there when she moved in, and the window curtains got in the way of the clothes. There was dead space above the cupboard, and it was a rather sad, tired room. With a little effort, it now works extremely well.

Stand back in your room and look up. More often than not, people forget to decorate and enjoy the high space in rooms. Here a full-length curtain and a bookcase over the mantelpiece add height to the room and a new concealed cupboard over the integral Victorian cupboard gives extra high storage. The fireplace, instead of being an unloved space, now works as a strong co-ordinating feature with the bookcase lined up above it. Behind the curtain in the wardrobe alcove there is now high shelving, and low shelving for shoes. A Roman blind at the window, instead of a curtain interfering with the clothes rail, pulls the room together.

With limited space and a small budget, the full-length curtain is an

LEFT: THE BEDROOM AS IT LOOKED BEFORE CLOTHES STORAGE ACTION.

ABOVE: GETTING RID OF THE MANTELPIECE AND MOVING EVERYTHING TO A BOOKCASE ABOVE LIFTS YOUR EYES OFF THE FLOOR AND INTO THE ROOM. THE FULL-LENGTH CURTAIN OVER THE CLOTHES IN THE ALCOVE COVERS EVERYTHING NEATLY.

effective way of hiding clothes and shoes. I've seen a whole wall of dress-rail covered by lengths of different coloured fabric sewn together and it looked wonderful. With the choice of fabrics around, you can create an individual look for little cost. We used a pretty muslin, but imagine leopard print fake fur or gold lamé.

LEFT: PREVIOUSLY, THE ORIGINAL VICTORIAN CUPBOARD JUST HAD A GAP ABOVE – WE NEED ALL THE SPACE WE CAN GET THESE DAYS.

BELOW: A MESSY, UNLOVED CUPBOARD WITH UNATTRACTIVE LOUVRE DOORS. IT NEEDS TO BE INCORPORATED INTO THE DESIGN OF THE WHOLE ROOM.

RIGHT: THE SIMPLE, NEAT BOOKCASE, FOLLOWING THE LINES OF THE FIREPLACE CUPBOARD UNDERNEATH, IS DESIGNED IN KEEPING WITH THE VICTORIAN ROOM. OLD FIRE-PLACES MAKE GREAT STORAGE SPACES.

Recessed cupboard

Not everyone wants to restore old fireplaces and particularly not in bedrooms, where you are unlikely to use them. If space is tight and you have an unused fireplace, think about turning the space into a useful cupboard. You don't need to remove the surround, merely make better use of the inside. The owner of this house keeps boxes of photographs and her child's treasured old toys in hers.

TIP

The magnetic catches – bought from hardware suppliers – mean that you don't have to have handles. The cupboards here use small ones for decoration.

YOU WILL NEED... *MDF cut to size • Panel moulding cut to size • Panel pins • Hammer • Wood glue • Acrylic wood primer • Four cabinet hinges • Screwdriver • Two magnetic door catches • Gloss or egg-shell paint*

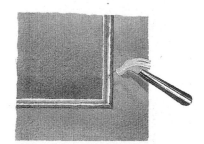

1 *Take the doors off the existing fireplace cupboard. Cut two new flush doors from MDF. Fix panel moulding, Victorian style, to the front of the doors, pinning and glueing it on. Prime the doors with acrylic primer.*

2 *Screw standard cabinet hinges to the new doors. These simply go on the edge of the doors without having to cut into them. Screw onto the wooden fireplace surround.*

3 *Hang the doors back in the space once occupied by the old doors. Use magnetic catches, which allow push action for both shutting and opening the doors. Paint the doors with either a gloss or egg-shell finish.*

Curtained wardrobe

This project is easy to do and covers all kinds of storage horrors. It can work equally well in a bathroom, hall, kitchen or bedroom and depending on the choice of fabrics, you can achieve a look from the simple to the sumptuous. Ready-made curtains can be bought in a variety of colours, textures and sizes or you can make your own. Choose your fabric carefully, bearing in mind how frequently you will need to get to the space.

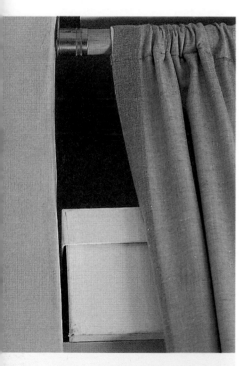

ABOVE: THE WARDROBE CURTAIN IN PLACE, REVEALING THE SCREW-IN COLLAR AND PLATE.

YOU WILL NEED... *Sufficient material, allowing 10% extra for shrinkage if to be washed • Length of 2 cm (¾ in) diameter dowelling pole • Brass plate, collar and rod end • Spirit level • Screws and screwdriver • Sewing needles and thread • Continuous lead weighting (optional)*

1 *To make the curtain, you will need length to fabric plus 24 cm (9½ in) for turnings, hems, etc. Double 25 mm (1 in) side hems and hemstitch in place. Put 22 gm (1 oz) of continuous lead weighting along the bottom if using fine muslin or similar material and stitch lightly at ends. Don't pull too tight or fabric will crease. At the top, turn over 10 cm (4 in) of fabric to allow for the dowelling pole and hemstitch into place.*

2 *Cut dowelling 25 mm (1 in) less than the width of the recess. Screw the rod end fixing to one wall, then check that the rod will be level using a spirit level and secure the plate to which the collar attaches into the other wall. The collar slides over the dowelling. To hang the curtain, slip the fabric over the dowelling pole. Insert the dowelling into the rod end, and screw the collar into the plate at the other side.*

Dressed Up

The couple who occupy this bedroom and office combined are animators and work part-time at home. In their work they use scalpels and other sharp instruments – not at all suitable for a room shared with a baby. They want to get as much as possible off the floor and away from inquisitive fingers. They were looking for ideas on how to stop the mess piling up and how to stay organized. Any solutions had to be quick and easy to achieve on a strictly limited budget and time scale.

Sandee Corshen is a New York storage guru with her own 'small space' ideas who came to help advise this couple. While they were keen to hear her ideas, they were quite resistant to being told how to restructure their lives. Like most of us, we know how the mess we live in works and someone else's philosophy on storage doesn't go down too well. They needed some persuading.

BELOW: THE COUPLE AND CHILD WHO LIVE HERE WORK AND SLEEP IN THIS ROOM. IT WAS CROWDED WITH CLOTHES, SHOES AND PAPERWORK. THEY WANTED SIMPLICITY FROM THEIR STORAGE.

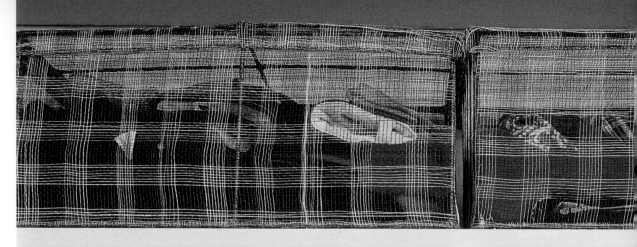

Sandee helped them to section off the room in their minds so that one area was for work, one for sleep and one for clothes. They were then to stick to their decision.

A quick and simple-to-maintain way to keep the possessions under control was to box them. Decorative boxes fit the shelf space above the shoes and, being see-through, allow the contents to be easily identified. If your boxes aren't transparent, clearly label what you put in them, otherwise you will have no idea what you've stored where and the boxes will be just as irritating as the original clutter.

Once the shoes had gone from under the bed, all the clothes not being used were put into large, secure boxes to

ABOVE: THE SPACE UNDER THE BED WAS HEAVING WITH SHOES AND LOOKED TERRIBLE. THEY WERE ATTRACTING DUST AND LOOKED UNCARED FOR.

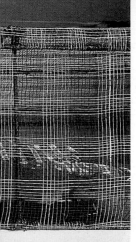

LEFT: SEE-THROUGH LIGHT-WEIGHT BOXES STORE GLOVES, SCARVES AND JEWELLERY. UNDERNEATH THERE'S A NEW SHELF WITH DIVIDERS TO HOLD ALL THE SHOES, WHICH NOW STAY NEAT, STACKED IN PAIRS, AND EASY TO FIND QUICKLY. THEY ARE PROTECTED FROM DUST, TOO.

systems easy to keep up. If they're too complicated, life will take over and you'll be back to clutter.

The storage guru provided the inexpensive solutions the couple needed, largely by simply getting everything off the floor and tucked into attractive boxes. She taught that extreme measures were not really necessary, and that storage problems are often solved by a bit of intelligent tidying up. Now all our couple have to do is to make sure they carry on putting things away!

protect them from dust, dirt, sunlight and moths. These were then labelled.

Clearing a space from under the bed is as good for your soul as it is for your shoes and other paraphernalia.

Clothes were put onto thin matching hangers which made more space on the rail and were hung the same way to make getting at them more straight-forward. Invest in a new set of hangers. It immediately smartens up your wardrobe and will keep your clothes in good condition.

All the work files, paper and filing cabinet were moved over to the desk area in the corner of the room. However small your room, it's worth separating your living and working space as best you can. And remember, make your

BELOW: OLD WOODEN FILING CABINETS LOOK GOOD ANYWHERE AND CAN BE USED FOR ALL KINDS OF STORAGE!

Children's Clothes

To keep anything to do with children in order demands non-stop work and re-ordering. It's impossible to keep their rooms looking as neat as they appear in these pictures. But the idea is to make your storage system so simple that it's easy to tidy up and, when the room is tidy, it looks good.

When you're decorating and organizing a child's room, remember to get down to their height. If your design is child-sized, it might convince the children to put their clothes and shoes away themselves.

I like the idea of a inexpensive school cupboard in a child's room. It's versatile and practical, and ones like this can be picked up surprisingly cheaply from secondhand office furniture suppliers. You can move a free-standing cupboard around as the children's needs change. It's not precious, so you can pin things

ABOVE: AN OLD WOODEN SCHOOL CUPBOARD HOLDS ALL THE CHILDREN'S CLOTHES AND MORE. BOOKS AND PUZZLES ARE KEPT IN THE CUPBOARD AT THE BOTTOM.

on it. Children can climb in the bottom cupboards and they can reach their own clothes. At the top, you can store sheets and towels out of their reach. As the children get bigger, you can rearrange the clothes to suit their height and quantity of clothing. It's also easy to see what's clean, unlike in a chest of drawers. Children's clothes are colourful and it seems a shame to hide them away.

The broom cupboard illustrated on the right has been divided into sections to suit the owner, who has three children with lots of shoes! Before, it was just a place to dump tennis rackets and old boots, with the space above wasted. With new child-high pegs, they can hang up their own coats, while shelves above hold other household bits and pieces which are out of their reach. Using a downstairs cupboard like this means that muddy wellingtons and wet anoraks don't find their way up to the bedrooms.

LEFT AND BELOW: A CONVERTED BROOM CUPBOARD IS USED HERE FOR ALL THE CHILDREN'S OUTDOOR CLOTHES. THE DOOR CLOSES SO THAT THE HALLWAY IS FREE FROM THE SIGHT OF THE CLUTTER IT CONTAINS.

LEFT: WHY NOT RECYCLE A SAWN UP OLD DOOR AS A DECORATIVE INSTANT SHELF? YOU CAN FIX THE ORIGINAL HANDLE UNDERNEATH THE BOTTOM SHELF TO USE AS A CLOTHES RAIL.

Collectables
and Clutter

Most of us collect something – books,
shells, children's art, pottery – and
whatever it is, we have to find a place
for it at home. Some people want to
display it, others hoard it away, content
to know they own it. Collections
usually have sentimental value and the
elements of it need to be cared for.
They remind us of who we are and so
they're very important.

BELOW: ONCE A BATHROOM, THIS BEDROOM MAY BE SMALL BUT IT'S BEAUTIFUL AND THE UNDER BED STORAGE MAKES THE BEST USE OF THE SPACE AVAILABLE.

Clutter Solutions

It's inevitable that the longer we live somewhere, the more we fill up our homes. Lack of storage space seems to be one of the commonest reasons for moving. Trying to accommodate all our personal things collected over the years gets harder as time goes on. All those photos, books, holiday purchases: where do you put them?

Look around at your home. Without impinging on your floor space, you can often create new cupboards above doors, along walls or cut into non-working fireplaces, and with a little organization of your possessions, you may not need to move as often or throw too much away.

ABOVE: THIS IS A CLEVER WAY TO MAKE FULL USE OF OVERHEAD SPACE. THE HALLWAY WAS EXTENDED INTO THE ROOM AND THE OVERHEAD CUPBOARD BUILT BACK INTO THE HALLWAY. THE RESULT: A BIGGER HALL FOR HANGING UP COATS AND A ROOMY TOP CUPBOARD IN THE BEDROOM.

LEFT: THESE FLOOR-TO-CEILING CUPBOARDS HAVE BEEN BUILT TO MAXIMIZE STORAGE AT ALL LEVELS — THE TOP CUPBOARDS FOR LITTLE-USED OBJECTS ARE A HOARDER'S DREAM.

To try and impose some order on your chaos, group whatever you collect and display it so as to create an impact. A random pile of shells gathering dust on a shelf looks nothing like as effective as when they are stored in a beautiful glass bowl. Suddenly they become treasured items and your eye can rest on them in a room. They're also much easier to dust!

With photos, magazine articles, paperwork and sentimental items that you want to keep but not display, a good old-fashioned box, carefully labelled and stored high up is the answer. Your possessions will be safe but won't interfere with your daily life. Give yourself time at the packing-up stage to throw out what you can bear to part with.

Try and find a special place for everything that you bring into your home. That way you will know where you keep the keys, the stationery, the photographs, and apart from having a tidier home, you will save yourself lots of time and anxiety endlessly looking for straying things.

It's worth making time for the occasional cull on everything in your home, so that the space you do have isn't taken up with items you no longer want or need. If you're like me this is the hardest part – I always wish I had never thrown out that old dress, that 1950s

ABOVE: VIRTUALLY ANYTHING BECOMES A FEATURE ONCE ITS DISPLAYED WELL – EVEN OLD MATCHBOOKS FROM YOUR TRAVELS.

RIGHT: A FABRIC THROW OVER A TABLE HIDES A LIBRARY OF BOOKS AND MAGAZINES AND WORKS WELL WITH THE MOOD OF THE ROOM.

clock, those priceless books. I can only advise that if your hoarding starts to get unbearable, then it doesn't matter that you have a few regrets as you stagger off to the dump. The extra space and liberation will more than make up for it. After all, dealing with storage is about getting to grips with your life and giving yourself some space in which to live it!

ABOVE: IF YOU NO LONGER HAVE A REAL FIRE, WHY NOT MAKE GOOD USE OF THE FIREPLACE FOR WINE STORAGE? PRACTICAL, ATTRACTIVE AND FUN AND THE DECORATIVE MANTEL SURROUND STAYS IN PLACE.

BELOW: NEW SHELF LIFE FOR AN OLD SCAFFOLDING PLANK LEFT BEHIND BY BUILDERS.

ABOVE: MAKE A STATEMENT WITH SHAPED, MULTICOLOURED SHELVES.

Shelves don't have to be boring, either. The recycled scaffolding plank looks lovely because it is so well weathered and unique. It is also sturdy enough to bear the weight of photo albums or art books. The shaped shelves on the left, fixed to a pillar at one end, are another clever idea, and make a collection of china and glass look really good.

Recycled wooden shelf

It's easy to turn what on first sight might appear to be a horrible old board into something with real character. Scour skips, salvage yards, sheds and your basement for old joists, etc. Don't be put off by rough condition. It's amazing what you can find that someone else has thrown away.

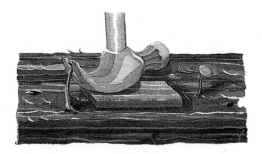

1 *Remove all nails from the plank or board. If you're pulling out nails with a hammer, use an old bit of wood underneath to protect the shelf. Timber yards can do this if you don't want to do it yourself.*

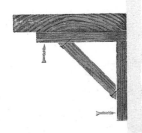

2 *Sand down, using an electric sander if possible. Stain, wax or varnish, depending on where the shelf is going, what it will be used for and how you want it to look.*

3 *Make sure when putting up shelves that you check whether the wall is solid or a cavity wall and use the correct screw and rawl plug for the job. Use a spirit level to make sure they are straight.*

4 *Choose brackets suitable for the wood. Simple home-made 45° wooden brackets under the shelf might suit. If storing heavy items, add a bottom batten cut on the diagonal. Screw into place.*

Stairwells and Hallways

Stairwells are often the most forgotten space in the home but with a little carpentry you can make them a focal point and create an extremely useful storage space as well. The chances are if you are lucky enough to have a stairwell in your home, you won't be using it efficiently. They're a great untamed space – even a simple high-level shelf displaying your favourite ornaments welcomes you into the home and is the perfect place to keep your breakables safe while on show. If your stairs are wide and the space well lit, you can really go to town and make a feature of your storage.

The hall and bottom of the stairs are usually the first place to drop things when you come home. And it's the first place you see when you go in. Mine are often full of anything from bicycles to endless pairs of kicked-off shoes, and, as you go up, books, magazines and cycle helmets.

The staircase is a thoroughfare to get to other parts, but it remains unused as an inventive place to put things. I think we just forget the stairs in the rush of day to day. But try and stop for a moment. Think how much better you would feel walking through your front door to a tidy hall and looking up to see some favourite object displayed up the stairs. See if your stairs are wide enough to build in some shelving alongside. Do you have any windows you could put glass shelves in front of to add interest?

LEFT: THIS DISPLAY OF TINS SITS WELL AGAINST THE TONGUE AND GROOVE BACKDROP. THE USE OF COLUMNS LIFTS YOUR EYE TO THE CEILING AND MAXIMIZES THE FEELING OF HEIGHT.

LEFT: A SIMPLE
SHELF ABOVE THE
LANDING PROVIDES
DRAMATIC HIGH-UP
DISPLAY SPACE FOR
YOUR TREASURES.

Make sure that whatever you decide
to do doesn't interfere with using the
stairs. The stairs area offers great
opportunities for displaying things, but
you do need to think carefully about how
to light them. So if it is books or
ornaments, try to get soft shelf lighting,
using movable small spots on the shelf or
from the ceiling. A whole staircase full of
books without proper lighting could end
up looking very oppressive, and you may
not be able to lay your hands on the
particular book you need.

ABOVE: A PERFECT STAIRCASE TO DISPLAY ANYTHING,
BECAUSE IT HAS TWO WINDOWS. PLANTS GROW WELL
HERE IN SUCH GOOD LIGHT.

LEFT: A LOW WALL IN THIS OPEN-PLAN HALLWAY
CREATES A PLACE FOR A USEFUL BENCH — AND
A HOME FOR SHOES. A TINY WALL CUPBOARD
ON TOP IS FOR STORING KEYS.

Books and Magazines

Order is what it is all about. With the hundreds of books and magazines so often stored at home, the aim is to control the potential chaos and be able to find what you need when you need it. Whether you go for simple bracket shelving or the sophisticated built-in units shown here doesn't matter. Get everything off the floor and onto the walls. If your rooms are big enough, use the space right up to the ceiling for shelving. It always seems odd that shelving tends to stop at door height when it can look extremely effective filling an entire wall. Judge this by your room. In some small rooms it could be oppressive, but if it works, it can add a substantial amount of extra space. Even if you don't use the extra height for books, it's useful for displaying hats and other items that are not often used.

ABOVE: IF YOU ARE DESIGNING YOUR SHELVING FROM SCRATCH, DO BUILD IN SOME HIDDEN CUPBOARDS. THAT WAY, ANY MESSIER ITEMS CAN BE STORED INSIDE, AND STILL GIVE YOUR ROOM THAT FEELING OF ORDER. DESPITE THE AMOUNT OF THINGS IN THIS ROOM, THE OWNERS RETAIN COMPLETE CONTROL OVER THEM. I TESTED THEM TO SEE IF THEY COULD FIND A PARTICULAR BOOK IN SECONDS. ABSOLUTELY NO PROBLEM! TRY TO ARRANGE BOOKS IN SUBJECT ORDER AND THEN ALPHABETICALLY WITHIN THESE SECTIONS. IT MAY SOUND PEDANTIC, BUT ONCE YOU HAVE DONE IT, YOU'LL NEVER LOSE ANOTHER BOOK.

LEFT: THE BOOKCASE AND CUPBOARD BUILT TO FIT THE SPACE IN THIS LONG CORRIDOR GIVE A DEAD SPACE SOME NEW LIFE.

Sound Systems

Since the launch of CDs in the early 1980s, every designer has had a go at designing storage for them, some more successfully than others. We've all seen the matt black towers, chrome high slats, the wooden boxes, the plastic, the metal, even the foam. I've even seen a neo-Georgian CD house. How far will it go?

RIGHT: JUST ONE EXAMPLE OF A HUGE SELECTION OF CD STORAGE OPTIONS, HERE IN BRIGHTLY COLOURED PLASTIC.

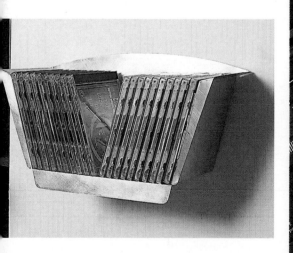

ABOVE: SIMPLE AND STYLISH, BUT ONLY FOR THOSE WITH A MINIMAL CD COLLECTION.

Album shelving

This is more complicated to build than some of the other projects but is an unusual way of dealing with all those old albums that you don't know what to do with. If you don't play them, they will look good, and if you do, it's very easy to find them!

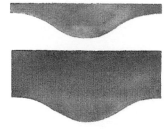

1 Decide on the shape for your albums. We chose a wave formation. Cut a template out of stiff cardboard with a scalpel.

ABOVE: A GREAT DESIGN FOR DISPLAYING YOUR OLD LPs THAT MAKES THEM LOOK LIKE A PIECE OF SCULPTURE. IT'S EASY TO FIND THE LP YOU WANT AND IT'S FAR MORE ATTRACTIVE THAN A ENDLESS LINE OF THEM. IT ALSO TAKES UP MUCH LESS SPACE.

2 Use shelving material wide enough to take the depth of an album (315 mm) (12 in) plus any additional width for your design, and strong enough to take the weight. We used 18 mm (¾ in) plywood. Use the template to cut out a shape which is 5 cm or 7.5 cm (2 or 3 in) wide at the narrowest point, using a jig-saw. Then cut out a second shape which is the width of the first plus 25 cm (10 in). This will mean that the albums extend out 5 to 7.5 cm (2 to 3 in) from the shelf, which is then not visible.

YOU WILL NEED... *Stiff cardboard • Scalpel • Plywood at least 18 mm (¾ in) thick cut to size • Jig-saw • Acrylic wood primer • Wood glue • Plywood battens • Screwdriver • Screws • Plywood uprights • Metal brackets • Electric drill • Rawl plugs*

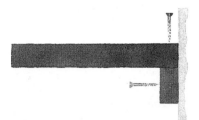

3 Glue the narrow shape on top of the full-width shape. This will give you a ridge at the back of your shelving to push the albums against and form a wave pattern.

5 We made 2 shelves for more effect and for more top storage. If doing this, you may need to support the top shelf with an upright or two, depending on the length of your unit. Cut the upright to extend no further than the raised section of the wave, or you will see it. If you need uprights, you should make the narrow wave form wide enough for the upright support to be effective. Attach the uprights with metal brackets, as shown.

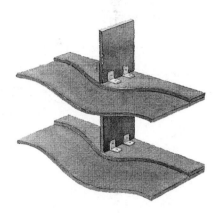

4 Fix a batten underneath each shelf with wood glue and screws so that you can attach the shelving to the wall more easily when your unit is finished. This will also help take the weight of the records.

6 The records slot in along the wave shape to give a curved line, and a flat shelf is here bracketed on to the top. Drill holes in the wall and screw the shelves onto the wall through the battens, making sure you use the correct rawl plugs.

Office Studies

Even if you have an office to go to, the chances are that you spend some of your time at home working.

As more and more of us struggle to work and relax in the same place, it becomes even more important to separate and organize that space effectively.

Working from Home

This is probably my favourite storage. The owner of the flat is an art director and fantastically conscious of space and order. It is one of the most inspiring uses of a small work space I have seen. Everything has its place and stays in it. It's a minute area in a small flat but it houses an amazing number of objects: magazines, books, tapes, papers, computer, lightbox and reference books. Just by looking at the space you know that the owner knows where every and any item is that he needs at any time. The desk is an efficient wooden surface which runs along two walls. Every bit of space counts, so there is no room for free-standing desks. Consider getting a desk like this built in if you are short of space. It frees up the space underneath the desk, which here is used for storing old magazines. Simple box files keep magazines tidy and make it easy to get at them for reference.

The shelving is designed specifically for the objects it holds. Unusually, most people don't think about the size of the books, tapes and videos they store and a lot of space is wasted by putting up shelves which are spaced too widely apart. Think about what you want to use your shelves for and make them the right depth and height. Despite the vast quantity of items in this office, they don't overwhelm you as they would in an unorganized space. Somehow, this office

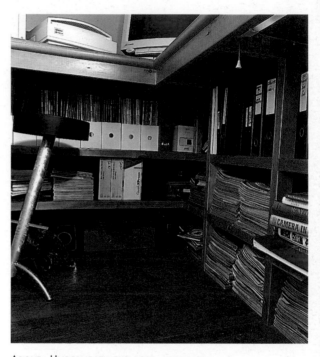

ABOVE: UNDERNEATH THE DESK, YEARS OF MAGAZINES ARE STORED IN DATE ORDER. BY USING BOXFILES, NO SPACE IS WASTED AND THE OVERALL EFFECT IS ONE OF ORDER.

oozes efficiency – you just know this person is in control of his work.

Even in this tiny room, the owner has managed to give the room a definite character. Most of the work he did himself and it has a very different feel from shop-bought shelving. Secondhand filing cabinets and an old chair, along with postcards and pictures, turn a functional room into a cosy haven to work in.

LEFT: THE WALL-TO-WALL DESK MAKES THE BEST USE OF THE SMALL SPACE. SHELVES OVERHEAD AND UNDER THE DESK NEATLY STACKED WITH REFERENCE BOOKS AND TAPES MEAN EVERYTHING IS TO HAND AND THE WORK ACTIVITY IS CONFINED TO ONE AREA.

RIGHT: PERHAPS THE BIGGEST TIP FROM THIS FLAT IS TO PLACE TOGETHER THINGS OF THE SAME HEIGHT — FOR EXAMPLE, TAPES AND VIDEOS. THIS CREATES VISUAL HARMONY, GIVING YOU A FEELING OF ORDER.

ABOVE: THIS IS NO RANDOM PLACING OF A PICTURE. SERIOUS SHELF SPACE HAS BEEN GIVEN UP FOR IT, BUT THE VISUAL IMPACT MAKES THE SACRIFICE WORTHWHILE. IT ALSO ALLOWS WORKING ROOM ABOVE THE INSET LIGHTBOX BELOW.

RIGHT: AN OLD OFFICE FILING CABINET FITS WELL INTO THIS INDIVIDUAL LOOK. SHALLOW DRAWERS ARE IDEAL FOR STORING PENS AND OTHER STATIONERY ACCESSIBLY. EACH DRAWER IS CAREFULLY LABELLED WITH ITS CONTENTS.

The success of this room is that is has not just evolved as random bits and pieces are added, but that it has been created from scratch as an efficient work area in a freelancer's house. It remains separate from the rest of his home so that his work does not spill out into all corners of his flat and take over his life. Somehow, the smallness of the space forces him to stay in control of his work and to store everything efficiently. Maybe this is a good lesson to learn. A large space allows you to be messy and lazy about your storage ideas. Even if you have got acres to play with, try to keep the ideas simple and keep them contained.

Unfortunately, there is still so much ugly office equipment that you have to have around you. If you can keep it to its own area, the grey lines of computers and faxes need not dominate the rest of your home.

ABOVE: NO SPACE IS WASTED HERE. THE OWNER BUILT THE SHELVING TO FIT HIS EQUIPMENT, WHICH INCLUDES SUCH AWKWARDLY SIZED OBJECTS AS A COMPUTER PRINTER AND FAX MACHINE.

THE PERSONAL TOUCH

As the owner has done here, try to vary the look you go for so that there is some old, some new and a sense that your home office is somewhere you are happy to work in. Even in this tight space, there is plenty of room for photos and personal items, which are very important. Most people work at home out of choice, and the office should maintain a better feel than it would if it was in a company building. Just because it is efficient, the work space does not have to be dull and boring.

Spare Room Study

This room is typical of many. It's a spare room that has to double as an office. Most of the time the office takes over, and as it wasn't designed as an office in the first place, the clutter starts to accumulate. Anne McKevitt designed this room for *Home Front*.

The most important task is to separate the work clutter from the personal papers. With personal books and papers sorted and placed in a new shelving unit in the corner (hidden by the striped roller blind), the room becomes businesslike and functional.

A plywood desk-top with a curved front was cut out with a jig-saw, giving enough space for two computer screens as well as a writing surface. Two old office filing cabinets were sprayed with enamel paint. All the paperwork was filed inside.

The wasted wall space above the desk was turned into more open shelving. This gives easy access for all the work reference books. It is important to think carefully about access when designing any storage. When working in a small

area, ask yourself before you start what you will need most from that particular space and make it work for you. If personal books had been stored on the shelf, the owner would have to leave her desk each time she wanted to refer to a work book. You would be amazed how many people waste so much time each day by keeping things in awkward places.

A new, sensible office chair, positioned at the right height for using the computer screens, completes the look and turns a nightmare work room into an organized and tidy office, with no anxious moments when that unexpected guest arrives to stay overnight!

RIGHT: A NEW SHELVING UNIT MEANS A CHANCE TO SEPARATE WORK AND PERSONAL BOOKS. LITTLE PEGS ON A LINE BENEATH THE BOTTOM SHELF KEEP IMPORTANT NOTES IN VIEW.

ABOVE: A NEW, SPACIOUS DESK GIVES
UNITY TO THE ROOM AND FILING CABINETS
TAKE ALL THE CLUTTER OFF THE FLOOR.

ABOVE: THE BEFORE SHOT, SHOWING THE
INADEQUATE WORK-TOP AREA AND STORAGE
SPACE. IT'S NEITHER A COMFORTABLE GUEST
ROOM NOR AN EFFICIENT OFFICE.

Working Life

To live and work in one room successfully it is important to try and separate the tasks you do in the room. The couple who own this flat had everything all over the place, as we saw on pages 21-3. The muddle was getting them down and made it far harder to get on with any work.

The solution was to give each corner of the room a function, with all the debris lying around consigned to one part of the room. Quickly and painlessly, the room came together. Cube shelves over the desk gave a distinctive and more artistic look to the room and proved very useful for storing things.

ABOVE: THE CUBES TAKE AWAY THE CLUTTER AND FREE THE DESK FOR ITS IMPORTANT JOB – WORK!

ABOVE: EVERYTHING WAS PILED HIGH ON THE DESK, WITH VALUABLE WALL SPACE UNUSED.
RIGHT: THE SIMPLEST IDEA – ADD AN EXTRA SHELF TO EXISTING SHELVING. MORE SPACE FOR MINIMUM ENERGY AND COST.

Cube shelving

This cube shelving makes more of an impact than standard shelving. It can be painted or stained for greater effect. Make sure you use the correct rawl plugs and drill bits for fixing. Plasterboard walls demand different fixings from solid walls.

ABOVE: CUBE SHELVING GIVES YOU THE OPPORTUNITY TO DISPLAY YOUR POSSESSIONS RATHER THAN MERELY STORE THEM.

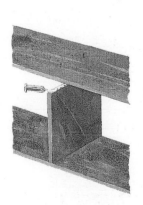

1 *To make the cubes, use 1 cm (½ in) standard interior plywood. For 8 cubes, cut two 240 cm (8 ft) by 25 cm (10 in) lengths of ply and then cut 9 dividers, each one measuring 30 cm (1 ft) by 25 cm (10 in). Fix the dividers to the two 240 cm (8 ft) lengths using panel pins and wood glue. Each cube measures 30 cm (1 ft) wide by 30 cm (1 ft) high by 25 cm (10 in) deep.*

2 *Fit a 5cm (2 in) by 2.5cm (1 in) batten on the inside top edge of each cube. Screw through the battens and into the wall to make the cubes secure. If storing heavy items, add a bottom batten cut at 45° to the wall on the outside edges of the end cubes. Varnish or wax the ply. A trim can be put on the cube's front face. Colour this by running a small paint roller along the edge of the cubes.*

Versatile Desks

The desk below is no desk – it's a dining-room table. It's often worth looking for an old table to change into a desk: they have a warm, comfortable feel to them and you can pick them up in junk shops pretty easily for much less than a new office desk. The problem comes in customizing your desk. Many second-hand filing cabinets are too big to fit underneath the table leaves. So check your table height and be prepared to search out cabinets of the right size. These new beech cabinets work well. Space is not at a premium in this office,

BELOW: MODERN AND TRADITIONAL FURNITURE SIT HAPPILY TOGETHER IN THIS SIMPLE, NO-FRILLS OFFICE, GIVING CHARACTER TO THE ROOM.

but if it was, perhaps a built-in desk around the bay window would have worked more efficiently. However, the look achieved is relaxed and homely.

As the office environment moves faster and faster towards consoles on communal desks, the plus of having your own desk at home is that there's still room for photographs and flowers to make it personal.

Whatever look you go for in your desk, make sure it feels comfortable and reflects you. The big advantage of working at home is you can do whatever you want with your space without someone telling you what you're allowed to do or not to do.

LEFT: ONE VARIATION ON THE LABELLING IDEA. CREATE A SIMPLE SHELF ABOVE THE DESK AND BUY OR MAKE BOXES. DECORATE THEM WITH RELEVANT PICTURES TO EASE THE SEARCH FOR PAPERWORK.

RIGHT: THIS 1950S DESK HAS A WONDERFUL LIFT-UP MIDDLE PANEL WHICH CONCEALS A BEAUTIFUL TYPEWRITER. BUT IT COULD ALSO ACCOMMODATE A COMPUTER SCREEN TO UPDATE THE IMAGE.

LEFT: IF YOU LIKE THE RETRO LOOK, FIND OLD FRUIT BOXES AT THE SUPERMARKET TO STORE YOUR PAPERWORK IN. SOME OF THEM HAVE THE MOST WONDERFUL COLOURS AND PICTURES. THEY ARE FREE, STURDY, STACK NEATLY AND LOOK GREAT.

Food and Drink File

Being able to see what you have and get at it easily is the most important aspect of storing both food and all your kitchen utensils. You only have to try to cook in a badly planned kitchen to realize that most people fail miserably with their storage.

Small Kitchen Spaces

The tiny kitchens here maximize the space available by using the full height of the rooms. Clever narrow shelves in the one below display everything. You have to be tidy for this look – and have a lot of good-looking china and pans! With careful planning, a small kitchen need not be a nightmare to work in. It is the room where you have the most things to house, but there is an infinite number of special kitchen storage devices around to help you. And sometimes, the smaller the space, the more organized you can become. A horizontal rail fixed along the front of a shelf will hold all your pots and pans at eye level and makes them easy to get at. A vertical pole gives you a chance to put in some random high shelving and makes an attractive feature of a small breakfast-bar table.

BELOW: WITH CAREFUL PLANNING, YOU CAN USE EVERY INCH OF ROOM, EVEN OTHERWISE DEAD SPACE OVERHEAD.

BELOW: YOU OFTEN SEE THIS SLEEK, HI-TECH
LOOK IN SHOPS BUT IT WORKS WELL IN KITCHENS,
ESPECIALLY WHEN SPACE IS TIGHT. THE SHELVES ON
THE POLE ARE NOT OPPRESSIVE.

Visibly Clean Lines

OK, most of us will never have a kitchen like this, but it does display ideas we can use in our more modest and probably messier homes. If you do any more than just warm up food in a microwave, then you need to have a clear work-top in your kitchen. Get things off the counter and into a cupboard.

ABOVE: THIS OWNER HAS PLENTY OF STORAGE AND IT SHOWS. LOOK AT THE VAST AND UNCLUTTERED WORK SURFACE — YOU CAN ACTUALLY COOK ON IT! I PROMISE YOU IT WASN'T TIDIED FOR THE PHOTO. THE REALLY AMAZING THING IS THAT IF YOU LOOK INSIDE THE UNITS, EVERYTHING IS TIDY THERE, TOO.

LEFT: SPECIALLY DESIGNED FOR THE SPACE, THIS GLASS-FRONTED CUPBOARD HAS EXCEPTIONALLY SHALLOW SHELVES SO THAT YOU CAN SEE EVERYTHING ON THEM. PROBABLY NOT DESIRABLE IF YOU ONLY HAVE 200 TINS OF BEANS IN YOUR CUPBOARD, BUT GREAT IF YOU HAVE A WIDE RANGE OF INTERESTING-LOOKING INGREDIENTS.

can find things easily, and a whole wall of them makes a dramatic impact in an otherwise bland space. But be warned: everything in them is visible and they will only look good if you have interesting food to display and are a naturally tidy person. Don't expect to change overnight from a 'push everything in the cupboard' sort of person to a neat one, although we can all work at it. Living up to the demands of glass cupboards could become a terrible burden if you are not dedicated to keeping up appearances.

This kitchen has been so well thought-out. The cupboards you can't see into are carefully organized and therefore simple to use. Everything has its own place, which does make life a lot easier. We all try to keep some semblance of order in our kitchens but cupboard space needs reviewing every so often. Check to see that you don't store the least used items in the most used cupboards.

The principle of having very shallow shelves where you can see all your groceries at a glance is a good one. Too often deep cupboards just hide lots of unused, out-of-date produce. These glass cupboards were designed so that you

LEFT: A SMALL RACK FOR KNIVES AND A HANGING RAIL FOR OTHER KITCHEN EQUIPMENT COMBINE DECORATION AND PRACTICALITY.

Kitchen pan rail

The pan rail is a device that works as well in a small flat as it does a farmhouse kitchen. This one is so simple to make – it's a matter of screwing a rail onto existing shelving. You can use chrome or stainless steel for the rail, depending on the look you want. Any good hardware shop will have swing hooks and will cut the rail to your needs. Check that your shelving is strong enough to support the pan rail and the pans, and shelves are thick enough to screw the swing hooks into without splitting (at least 2 cm or ¾ in).

1 *Use 38 mm (1½ in) diameter chrome-plated, brass or stainless steel tubing. Cut this to size using a small hacksaw. File off any jagged edges. Attach the pan rail to the shelving using swing hooks. These come in 7.5 cm or 13 cm (3 in or 5 in) galvanized steel from any good hardware shop.*

2 *You will need to ease open the swing hooks with a vice to get the pan rail inside as they're normally used for hanging things like hammocks. Drill small guide holes at regular intervals along the edge of the shelf and screw in the swing hooks. Slot through the pan rail, starting from one end. Hang your pots and pans from the rail using meat hooks.*

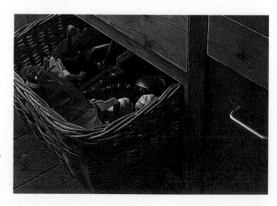

RIGHT: A BASKET FOR VEGETABLES ALLOWS THEM TO BREATHE AND TUCKS AWAY LIKE A DRAWER.

ABOVE: POTS AND PANS HANG
FROM MEAT HOOKS ON THE
FINISHED RAIL. IT LOOKS BETTER IF
YOU KEEP THE OUTSIDES OF YOUR
PANS SHINY CLEAN!

RIGHT: EVERY INCH OF WALL
SPACE IS USED HERE AND
STILL LOOKS GREAT.

Rustic Recycling

What I like about this kitchen is the ingenuity of the ideas. Everything you see on these two pages is recycled from old wood. Search it out in skips and junk yards. Some of the wood used here came from old doors and table tops, which you can often pick up cheaply in secondhand shops. Most timber yards will cut wood to size and plane it for you, saving you a lot of hard work.

Apart from the obvious cost advantage, there's a satisfaction in knowing that recycled wood has a history and that units made from it often

BELOW: ONE OF THE SPINDLES IN CLOSE-UP – YOU CAN FIND THESE SECONDHAND OR HAVE MADE ANY DESIGN YOU FANCY.

ABOVE: A CHEAP AND CHEERFUL DRESSER MADE OF RECYCLED SHELVES W MODERN TURNED SPINDLES FOR DECORATIVE DETAIL AND AS SUPPORTS. IF HAVE THE CARPENTRY SKILLS, THIS COSTS ALMOST NOTHING TO MAKE.

look better than a brand-new kitchen.
You can use the wood for shelves, work-
tops and cupboards. Making shelving is
not all that difficult, though cupboards
underneath the sink like those shown
here are a bit more tricky.

The dresser has always been a great
place to hide everything while still
looking beautiful – my idea of heaven.
For an instant tidy-up you can sling
things inside its vast cupboards and
drawers and no-one will know what
chaos hides inside. All you see is the
decorative arrangement of plates on the
shelves. People often pay a fortune for a
ready-made new or antique kitchen
dresser. But if you make your own, the
look will cost you little more than putting
up a few shelves and you can decorate it
in exactly the same way as a traditional
dresser, perhaps with classic blue and
white china.

LEFT: MADE FROM AN OLD TABLE, THE BASE OF
THE DRESSER PROVIDES VALUABLE EXTRA CUPBOARD
AND DRAWER SPACE IN THE KITCHEN.

ABOVE: THIS LOVELY OLD CUPBOARD WITH LATTICED DOORS HAS THE BEST OF BOTH WORLDS – YOU CAN SEE THE GROCERIES BUT NOT HOW TIDY THEY ARE!

Free-standing Pantry

If you don't have a built-in pantry in your kitchen, think of the possible alternatives that might work. This huge cupboard stores everything from spices to jams in its cavernous depths. You may choose something smaller to suit the room, but think about furniture that isn't necessarily made for the kitchen. There are all kinds of interesting ethnic-style cupboards around from Mexican to Moroccan. (I know someone who has a Turkish peanut-stallholder's cart in her kitchen to store all her spices in – original, and it works.) But beware the purely decorative and unsuitable. There's nothing more irritating than a piece of furniture that takes up valuable space but doesn't do its job properly.

ABOVE: OPEN SHELVING IN THE CORNER OF A KITCHEN ALLOWS YOU TO TURN YOUR RICE AND BEANS INTO A DECORATIVE STATEMENT.

LEFT: A VERY LARGE WOODEN WINE RACK STORES YOUR BOTTLES CORRECTLY AND MAKES IT EASY TO PICK OUT THE ONE YOU WANT – NOT A GOOD IDEA IF THERE ARE TODDLERS AROUND, THOUGH!

When you find your ideal cupboard, try and keep it in order. Have sections for jams, oils, sugars and spices. Use adjustable-height inner shelves and lots of labelling. Take foodstuffs out of their packaging and store them in jars and containers. This keeps insects out and makes things easier to find. When I sorted out my cupboard I even found the experience enjoyable. And I managed to throw out a lot of odd buys that had been lurking around unopened for years. It's a false economy to buy some dry stores in bulk, especially spices. They go off long before you can use them up and large quantities take up precious space in your cupboards.

BELOW: SEE-THROUGH BASKETS KEEP AWKWARD PACKETS NEATLY CONTAINED AND MAKE IT QUICK AND EASY TO IDENTIFY THE CONTENTS. THE DRAW THEN SLOTS AWAY BEHIND CLOSED DOORS.

ABOVE: CO-ORDINATE THE DRINKS AND TELEVISION CUPBOARD IN YOUR SITTING ROOM WITH YOUR OTHER FURNISHINGS BY SIMPLY LINING THE WIRE-MESHED DOORS WITH FABRIC. THIS IS SURPRISINGLY EASY TO DO.

Fabric-lined doors

Cupboards hide a multitude of evils! Ugly televisions, endless bottles, toys, china – if you want to hide it away yet be able to access it easily, fabric adds instant life to pieces of furniture that can be rather plain, dark and dominating. The wire-meshed doors of this cupboard are ideal for the treatment.

YOU WILL NEED...
Curtain or upholstery fabric • Sharp scissors • Staple gun • Ribbon or braid • Upholstery stud pins • Hammer (optional)

TIP

Heavier fabrics will work better than lightweight ones, which will look flimsy. You need something thick enough to make sure you can't see the contents of the cupboard through it.

1 *Measure the space to be covered and add 4 cm (1½ in) all around. Cut out the fabric to those measurements. Fold the rough edges of the fabric over and staple it on around the inside edge of the door.*

2 *Buy enough ribbon or braid to cover the edges of the fabric. This will hide all the staples. We used 4 cm (1½ in) petersham ribbon. Pull the ribbon taut and hammer in the decorative upholstery stud pins in each corner. These are available at any haberdashers.*

Bathrooms *and Laundry*

However small your bathroom,
it has to do so much. Every inch of
space is needed for laundry, loo rolls
and medicines, yet we choose to
decorate it with exotic perfume bottles
and sweet-smelling oils. It must still
be a sanctuary and a place to shut
out the world and relax in.

Laundry

Laundry isn't attractive stuff, on the whole. Unless you tumble-dry everything, which does terrible things for your electricity bill and not much for your clothes, most of us have it hanging around somewhere. Whether you live in one room or have space to hide it, you can make it more fun to live with.

I know someone with six children who has her laundry really well organized. Everything happens in one small room. If you can, put your washing machine on the same floor as your bedroom. That way, you eliminate all that moving around. Simply take your clothes off, put them in the laundry basket, then wash, dry and iron them all in the same space. It will take years off your life! If you have room, use two baskets – one for colours and one for whites – and train the family to sort their washing.

ABOVE: THIS WELL-ORGANIZED LAUNDRY CORNER HAS EVERYTHING – BASKETS, SHELVES AND A WORK-TOP.

STYLISH DRYING

Hanging a line over the bath is an age-old way of drying your washing and is the obvious place if space is limited. Hotels, for instance, have the simple pull-out wire which nearly garottes you when you forget to release it before you get in the bath. Then there are the wonderful old-fashioned wooden driers which traditionally hung above the Aga or Raeburn in a farmhouse kitchen. They've become more popular again and mail-order catalogues are selling modern reproductions. Whether this means it's now fashionable to display your laundry I'm not sure, but the pulley system opposite is a modern and colourful variation on the theme.

RIGHT: A MARINE PULLEY SYSTEM GIVES A WHOLE NEW LOOK TO HANGING YOUR CLOTHES OVER THE BATH TO DRY.

Ship-shape pulley system

The purpose of this pulley system is to make a feature of your airing space. All the fittings used are from a specialist marine supplier which adds to the fun of the look. The rope and pulley come from Pumpkin Supplies (see Sources, page 94) and you can send for them mail order, or try any marine supply shops for a similar look. The pulleys we used are called 'upright blocks'. These have springs at their base which allow for movement on a ship, but this does means that they will stand out at an angle which will vary according to the tension applied. The pulley system will also work perfectly well with fixed, non-spring-loaded pulleys as illustrated below.

YOU WILL NEED...
Pulley system as below • Nautical rope • Strong metal hooks • Power drill • Screwdriver • Standard cleat hook

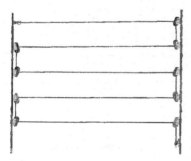

1 *Work out how many pulleys and how much cord you need for your space. Start at the wall where the line begins and attach a strong hook to the wall. Fix securely, as the cord will be pulled taut. Tie cord on.*

2 *Attach an upright pulley at each turn of the cord. Since the lines should be equally spread and parallel, check carefully where each pulley should be attached. Get some friends to hold the pulleys in place to check their position*

under tension before you drill holes to screw them to the wall. To fix the end of the cord, simply buy a standard cleat hook and wind the cord around it. Now you can hang up your knickers!

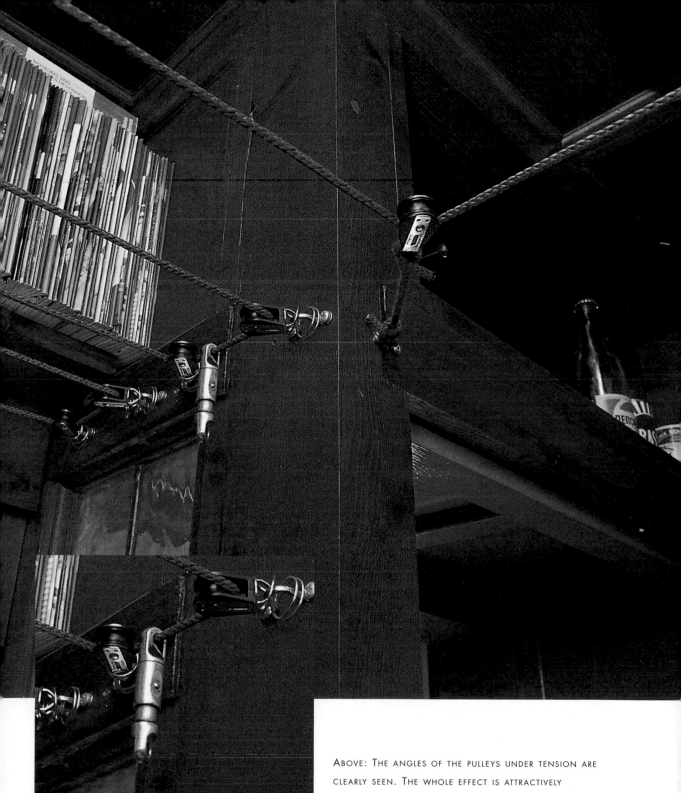

ABOVE: THE ANGLES OF THE PULLEYS UNDER TENSION ARE
CLEARLY SEEN. THE WHOLE EFFECT IS ATTRACTIVELY
NAUTICAL, A BRILLIANT WAY OF ELEVATING A WASHING LINE
TO A MUCH HIGHER STATUS!

LEFT: THE SPRING-LOADED PULLEY, AT A 45° ANGLE.

FINDING A SPACE

Space to do the washing in is always going to be limited. Unless you live in a rambling mansion, any decent-sized room will be devoted to living in. So you need to think about how best to use any odd available space.

Hanging up wet washing in the house is messy and unsightly and gets worse as children come along. How many radiators have you seen draped with little babygros or old socks? Keep the washing to one area if possible. If you have a boiler, it's worth building a simple structure around it to use for drying clothes. Even if this doesn't run to a full-blown airing cupboard, it will give you some hidden space for the purpose. Use high up areas for drying. If you're

ABOVE: UNDER THE STAIRS IS A GOOD PLACE TO STORE CLEANING PRODUCTS, IRONING BOARD AND PERHAPS A COLLAPSIBLE CLOTHES HORSE.

ABOVE: A HIGH RAIL FOR DRYING CLOTHES HAS BEEN ADDED TO THE DEAD SPACE ABOVE THE SINK IN THIS UTILITY ROOM.

short of room, collapsible drying horses are useful.

Laundry baskets are fun enough to be kept on display now, in a bedroom or a child's room. There are fold-away ones, brightly coloured plastic ones or the more traditional wicker shapes. You can even get corner ones which work well next to the washing machine. There is no excuse for a tacky dirty laundry basket. Preferably, go for one with a lid, as it hides all the horrors.

When you do the laundry, it should be as pleasurable as possible. The main thing you need to make room for in the a laundry room is a radio!

ABOVE: IN THE COUNTRY WITH ROOM TO DANCE WHILE YOU IRON. THE TRADITIONAL HANGING CLOTHES DRIER IS PROBABLY MORE FOR EFFECT HERE, THOUGH USEFUL ON RAINY DAYS: THERE'S PROBABLY A CLOTHES LINE IN THE GARDEN.

LEFT: ONE OF THE ALL TIME GREAT DESIGNS. THE CLOTHES HORSE HAS BEEN AROUND FOR EVER. DESIGNERS ARE NOW ALSO COVERING IT WITH DECKCHAIR CANVAS AND USING IT FOR STORAGE.

BELOW: BE CAREFUL WHEN YOUR CUPBOARDS ARE AS BIG AS THIS. IT'S EASY TO LOSE TRACK OF WHAT YOU HAVE. TRY AND DESIGNATE SHELVES FOR SPECIAL PRODUCTS AND USE BOXES AND BASKETS INSIDE TO KEEP THINGS ORGANIZED.

Hanging glass shelves

First, decide if glass shelves are right for your space. They are most suitable for displaying light, decorative objects. Measure the width for the shelves. If this is more than about 60 cm (2 ft), check with your glass supplier to see if glass is suitable. Ask advice on the thickness of the glass. You should never get shelves less than 8 mm (¼ in) thick. Then decide on the look – perhaps a wavy edge, opaque glass, or etched with a design. And remember to get the edges polished.

LEFT: GLASS SHELVES COME INTO THEIR OWN IN A BATHROOM. USE THEM PURELY FOR LIGHTWEIGHT DECORATION AS GLASS IS TOO HEAVY TO TAKE WEIGHTY OBJECTS.

YOU WILL NEED...
Pencil • Plumbline • Spirit level • Electric drill • Rawl plugs • Screwdriver • Screws • Decorative brackets • Glass as described opposite

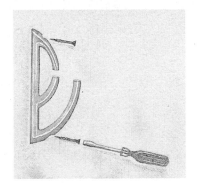

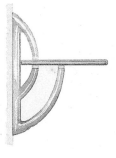

1 Mark up the drill holes checking that they are vertical with a plumbline and level with a spirit level. Drill and plug the holes with rawl plugs. Make sure you use the correct rawl plugs and drill bit for the wall you're working on.

2 Fit the brackets on a wall which will take the weight of the glass. Hollow plaster-board walls need special butterfly plugs to hold shelves secure. You should try and find the wood frame supporting the plasterboard to screw into.

3 Place brackets no more than 40 cm (16 in) apart. Put the screws through the brackets and screw to the wall. Choose decorative brackets like the ones illustrated here, as they are as visible as the shelves.

ABOVE LEFT: UNITS LIKE THESE MADE FROM INEXPENSIVE KITS MAKE THE MOST OF THE SMALLEST SPACES AND WILL FIT ALL SHAPES OF ROOM – CHILDREN LOVE THEM.

ABOVE RIGHT: BASKETS ARE A QUICK AND EASY WAY OF GETTING TOYS UP FROM UNDERFOOT.

BELOW LEFT: TURN A SIMPLE SHELVING UNIT INTO A TOY CASTLE.

BELOW RIGHT: ADD SOME COLOUR AND SMALL CUPBOARD DOORS AND YOU MAY ENCOURAGE YOUR CHILDREN TO PUT THEIR TOYS AWAY.

Room *for* *the* Children

I'm probably beating my head against a brick wall with this chapter. Toys live everywhere and never in boxes stacked neatly in cupboards (unless you put them there). My advice here is not to set yourself too high a target – it's not so far to fall. Oh, and enjoy yourself while you're trying to get organized. If your ideas are fun, you may get the children interested in following your example.

Crafts Cupboard

Every home has dead space where junk gathers. If you have children, this just gets worse, and worse, and worse. Take stock of where it all ends up. Then work out if certain things end up in the same place. This crafts cupboard is a good example of an area which was used for paper, paints, glues etc. It was near the sink and a wooden floor made a good area for painting. The space was crying out for a crafts cupboard. Making doors for the cupboards is a good idea with all the different items being stored. It is less messy and doesn't impose on the overall effect of the kitchen. Painting it a bright colour gives a dead corner a new identity and draws children to play there.

If building a cupboard yourself is too much to take on, think about hiring a carpenter to build some storage for you. It needn't cost a fortune and it does make the most use of an unusual space. Any number of free-standing units could have been bought for this area but none would have used the space so effectively. Thinking of a design to fit a space also focuses your ideas on what you want out of it and what will work.

LEFT: DIFFERENT SIZES OF DRAWERS DESIGNED TO SEPARATE ACTIVITIES AND ENCOURAGE CHILDREN TO EXPLORE. THEY QUICKLY LEARN WHAT GOES WHERE — WHETHER IT ACTUALLY GOES IN THERE IS ANOTHER STORY.

ABOVE: MESSY AND UNUSED
SPACE NEXT TO A FRIDGE.

LEFT: A MODERN CUPBOARD
DESIGNED TO FILL THE SPACE.
THE TALLER CUPBOARDS ALLOW
STORAGE FOR MEDICINES AND
OTHER LESS CHILD-FRIENDLY
ITEMS. DOORS OPEN USING
PUSH CATCHES, AND DRAWERS
HAVE SIMPLE GEOMETRIC
SHAPES SUITABLE FOR LITTLE
HANDS TO OPEN. ALL THE
PAINTS, PAPER, BRUSHES,
GLUE, SCISSORS, PLASTICINE,
STICKY SHAPES ARE IN THEM.

High-rise Living

Children often prefer small bedrooms even if you have the luxury of space. They are cosier and easier to create secret worlds in. I think what little floor space is available should be kept free for play, which means everything else goes up or under. If you are buying a child's bed, try and get one with enough space underneath for storage. You can combine hiding games and hiding boxes full of toys. A bunk-bed like the one in the picture is the perfect answer for slightly older children, even if you only have one bed. It makes bedtime fun and gives you double the storage space. A built-in corner seat keeps floor space free of chairs and gives you another chance for drawers underneath.

Coloured plastic boxes are almost obligatory. While you can get overwhelmed with yellow, red and blue plastic when you have children, it has its positive plus points. It's cheap, tough and waterproof. Don't buy cute but expensive painted chests – two years on they will hate them. Keep it simple and

ABOVE: A QUIET READING CORNER – COSY WITH HIGH AND LOW LEVEL STORAGE. THE BOXED-IN CUPBOARDS BELOW ARE GIVEN CUSHIONS AND THE AREA IS NICELY ENCLOSED.

LEFT: EVERYTHING YOU COULD POSSIBLY NEED IN THE TINIEST OF SPACES. A TOTALLY FLEXIBLE KIT FOR GROWING CHILDREN. THE AREA UNDERNEATH THE SINGLE BUNK-BED IS DESIGNED TO INCORPORATE A LITTLE DESK. HANG A CURTAIN FROM UNDER THE MATTRESS AND IT BECOMES A DEN.

versatile and think of your child and not of yourself when making decisions on storage. A shelf or peg at adult height means more work for you and does nothing to encourage your child to tidy up. The best schemes combine function and fantasy – it is no good having everything neatly stored if it just looks boring.

Castle toy cupboard

Making a cupboard like this encourages children to put their toys away, especially if they have their own child-sized doors. We chose MDF for the cupboards as it's cheap and we were painting them. You can get big sheets of MDF 240 cm by 48 cm (8 ft by 4 ft) but it's heavy and it's hard to cut straight edges on it with ordinary tools. It's best to go to a timber yard who will cut everything to size. The various doors need to be attached to shelving already fixed in position. Make sure you measure it carefully. Carpenters have an old and useful phrase carved into their brains – measure twice, cut once.

RIGHT: THE TOY CUPBOARD IS COMPLETELY FUNCTIONAL BUT GREAT FUN TOO. WITH THIS MANY DOORS AND NOOKS AND CRANNIES, CHILDREN WILL ACTUALLY ENJOY TIDYING UP THEIR TREASURED POSSESSIONS.

YOU WILL NEED...

MDF cut to size • Acrylic wood primer • Electric drill • Jig-saw • Softwood strips • Wood glue • Small metal hinges • Screwdriver • Cranked hinges • Wood plane • Touch latches • Magnetic catches • Medum grade sandpaper • Paints

1 Use 12mm MDF for the basic cupboard doors. Make a template or draw a shape directly on to the MDF for the mini gate. Cut out with a jig-saw. Attach the doors to an existing shelving unit. Prime with an acrylic primer before assembly.

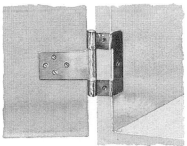

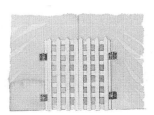

4 The hinges for the main doors are cranked hinges. These allow you to fit the doors onto the front of the shelving and still have them open fully, which a standard cabinet hinge would not.

2 Our windows in the middle of the upper doors were cut with a jig-saw after drilling a pilot hole to get the blade of the saw through the boards. The parapet was also cut with a jig-saw.

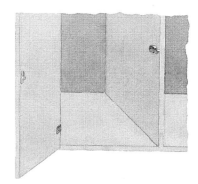

6 Fix touch latches on the big doors for a smooth finish. To open, press once, and again to shut. They are a bit fiddly to position but useful for this type of project. Use magnetic catches for the small doors. Rub down the cut edges of the MDF with sandpaper and a block of wood to eliminate any saw marks that may show. Paint carefully. Use strong primary colours for dramatic effect.

3 To make the gates at the bottom, use thin, flat softwood strips which you can find in several different sizes in any timber shop. Assemble using wood glue and fix onto the bottom doors using the smallest hinges possible.

5 You might need someone to help hold the doors for you while you mark the position of the hinges, adjusting them if necesssary or planing a little off the doors. Make sure the pairs of doors are at the same height and have an even gap between them if you can.

Basements *and Sheds*

If you have a basement or a shed these are likely
to be the places where you are truly revealed.
Are you that organized person with things in boxes,
or more likely the person who throws items inside,
in the vain belief you will deal with them later?
If you are the latter, let me reassure you – the space
you're dealing with is usually quite small and it
is possible to get to grips with it – but you have to
take everything out and start again!

Hang Up That Clobber

When I didn't have a basement, I longed for one. The idea of having a space to store all those things you may need one day was bliss. Now I have one, I dread going into it. It has got all those things I will never need in it. And there's always a million reasons I can think of why I haven't got time to clear it out. Basements are, of course, hidden spaces, but only to other people. You know they are there and you know what they hide.

They can be incredibly oppressive if you don't take them in hand.

This basement was a horrible mess and the owner kept meaning to sort it out. It was my offer to sort it for her that geared her into action. And when we started, it really didn't take that long. It was full of the usual paint cans and a whole pile of work tools but had no space in which to use them. I think you should always enlist help to crack a basement.

To start with, a simple hook or two screwed into the wall gets the top of the stairs uncluttered. When you open the door and come face to face with mops and bags waiting to trip you up, it discourages you from venturing any further down. Paint the stairway a strong colour – this will make you feel better about the space and give it an identity rather than it being a dark hole. Get some simple lighting fixed to make sure you can see easily when you are in there. So many basements are gloomy – remember that the brighter the better.

LEFT: TYPICAL OF BELOW THE STAIRS – THAT DEPRESSING WASTED SPACE AND STUFF EVERYWHERE WAITING TO TRIP YOU UP.

LEFT: KEEP THE
BRUSHES AND MOPS
WITHIN EASY REACH
AND STORE LESS
DAY-TO-DAY STUFF
FURTHER DOWN THE
STAIRS. HERE
PROGRESS HAS
ALREADY BEEN MADE
BY GETTING STUFF
UP ONTO THE WALL.

ABOVE: EXPENSIVE
SPORTS EQUIPMENT
WHICH IS USED
ONLY OCCASIONALLY
NEEDS TO BE OUT
OF THE WAY, BUT
LOOKED AFTER.
HANG IT UP FOR
SAFETY.

Work out what you use most in your basement. Here it is wine, paint and tools, so they should be accessible. Check whether your basement is dry or not. If it isn't, don't put your china and fabrics down there.

Recycled wood is ideal for building shelves in basements as its age adds to the atmosphere. Even if you are a beginner in carpentry skills, the basement is as good a place as any to try out your handiwork. And just by looking around in skips and salvage yards you will find enough wood to do

all you need. The final result will be sturdier than many of the cheaper shelving units you may buy for a basement and will be all your own work. The owner of this basement enjoys doing carpentry but had nowhere to make things. An unused wall of the basement makes a perfect bench for working on. The pegboard is simply nailed to the wall and special hooks placed on it to hang tools from. It looks good and the tools are easy to use.

A dry basement is essential if you are planning to store tools in such an open display. The best storage in the world will be ruined if the damp gets to your things. Even if the basement is dry, don't store boxes on the floor, use bricks or pallets to allow the air to circulate.

ABOVE: MORE CLUTTER TO BOX UP.

When you box things up, make sure you wrap them well and label everything clearly. You may not open the box for some time. It's worth doing a quick coat of white emulsion over the walls to jolly up the space, especially if you plan to work in it.

BELOW: A WORKBENCH AND PEGBOARD WHICH MEAN THE BASEMENT'S IN BUSINESS. THIS IS NOW ANOTHER USABLE ROOM RATHER THAN JUST A JUNK PLACE.

The Garden Shed

I love sheds. There's something so other worldly about them. Men on the whole dominate shed culture, as it's that surreal escape hole at the bottom of the garden where no one can get you. Most sheds start off with good intentions and have places for nails, flower pots, lawn-mowers, but get overrun when they have to accommodate all the other things you have no idea what to do with in your home, such as children's bikes, foldaway chairs, tools, brushes, paint pots, fertilizer bags – the list is endless for the poor old shed.

Before you start cramming endless items in your shed, I think a good clear out works wonders. So many things get thrown in sheds that you will never need or even want again that it is worth that initial trip to the dump before you start to organize. I don't say that lightly, I like to keep most things but sheds are *small* spaces.

The crucial thing is to use the wall space. Often sheds make no use of the walls and they are perfect for high level storage. You can put all those child unfriendly items out of harm's way, leaving the lower part of the walls for hanging up

garden implements. Get plenty of hooks on the walls at suitable heights for all your gardening tools. It looks good and you'll be able to get at them easily.

Anything put in a shed should be carefully thought about. Bicycles shouldn't be stored so far back that you never want to get the bike out because it is so much hassle. Keep the bikes in front of the lawn-mower and put the old fertilizer bags at the back. You don't want to spend your time climbing over things you only use on the odd gardening weekend.

ABOVE: THE TYPICAL GARDEN SHED, STUFFED FULL OF JUNK AND IMPOSSIBLE TO GET INTO.

LEFT: THIS SHED NEEDS SERIOUS SORTING, NOT TO MENTION SEVERAL TRIPS TO THE DUMP.

BELOW: NOW THIS IS WHAT I CALL A LOVELY SHED, ROOM TO MOVE AND TO DISPLAY YOUR WARES. AND IT INCORPORATES A COLLAPSIBLE POTTING BENCH.

If you haven't much space, leave the door off, then you can get those awkward bicycles in. You can buy sheds off the peg in all kinds of sizes, from ones you can hardly get into to luxury rooms at the bottom of your garden. I have a friend who built a two-storey shed to watch the television in as his girlfriend didn't approve of watching TV. You may not want to go that far with your

designs, but do think about what you want your shed for. Is it a hideaway at the bottom of the garden to do your favourite hobby in or do you just want to store all those things that will go rusty if you don't?

If you are buying or building it from scratch, build the biggest one you will need for your things. Try and get some natural light in it with a velux or build in a window. That way, it becomes its own little place and not an old box at the end of the garden.

Try and think positively about the shed and don't let it become a dumping ground for things you don't know what to do with. If you look after it and keep it tidy, it will be a pleasure to use your tools and enjoy your garden. If you have to wade through tea chests of semi-discarded junk, you'll never get the gardening done.

Old chests of drawers and small shelving units from junk shops work brilliantly in sheds. You can leave them in their rough state, in keeping with the natural, relaxed feel of the garden. They

are great for all the small details of gardening such as seeds, wire, nails and string. It's worth labelling the drawers clearly – it makes planting so much easier when you know which bulbs are which!

Now that people buy garden accessories from design shops as well as from garden centres, there are so many extras you can kit your shed with. You can get everything from suede hanging aprons with multiple pockets to beaten tin and wood drawers. There is no reason why your shed, while doing its job, shouldn't look as good as your sitting room if that's the way you like it.

Just a thought if you want to go for a shed in a big way. I've just met a young man who has turned his tiny shed in his mum's garden into a neo-classical retreat with cherubs, chandelier and central heating. Not a trowel in sight. The creative possibilities are endless.

ABOVE: A DOORLESS BRICK SHED WITH PLANTING CONTAINERS ON TOP TO ADD TO ITS RURAL CHARM. UNSIGHTLY THINGS ARE STORED AT THE BACK AND BICYCLES CAN BE WHEELED IN AND OUT ACROSS THE PATIO.

RIGHT: A SHOP-BOUGHT, STURDY SHELVING UNIT IS WORTH BUYING FOR THE SHED IF YOUR OWN CARPENTRY SKILLS ARE LIMITED TO JUST SCREWING THE FLAT-PACKED PARTS TOGETHER.

Sources

Guy Tortora – designer and maker of bespoke fitted furniture and storage on Tel: 0181 340 5366

Giles Leaman – carpenter and expert wood reclaimer on Tel: 0181 983 1109

Rita Lovell – soft furnishings on Tel: 0181 806 7304

Nishma Chandé – designer on Tel: 0171 586 1169

Jam – designers on Tel: 0171 278 5567

Emily Mason – wild clay pots on Tel: 0171 733 1020.

Storage comes in many guises – if you're planning to create your own, think skips, timber yards, glass merchants, salvage yards, junk shops and hardware stores.

Mail order companies include:
Pumpkin Marine and Leisure Ltd for the ship-shape pulley system on Tel: 0171 480 6630; Muji on Tel: 0171 494 1197; Aeromail on Tel: 0181 971 0066; The Holding Company on Tel: 0171 352 1600; McCord Design on Tel: 0990 535455; Lakeland Limited on Tel: 015394 88100; The Shaker Shop on Tel: 0171 724 7672.

Other stores include:
After Noah on Tel: 0171 359 4281; Aria on Tel: 0171 704 1999; The Futon Company; Habitat;

BBC Books would like to thank the following for providing photographs and for permission to reproduce copyright material. While every effort has been made to trace and acknowledge all copyright holders, we would like to apologize should there be any errors or omissions.

PICTURE CREDITS

Pages 2 & 3 Robert Harding Picture Library (Steve Dalton/Options); Page 5 Robert Harding Picture Library (Polly Wreford/Homes and Gardens); Page 6 Richard Kendal © BBC; Page 7 The Bridgeman Art Library (Lauros-Giraudon); Page 13 McCord Design top right; Page 27 Robert Harding Picture Library (Steve Dalton/Options) bottom left; Arcaid (Trevor Mein) tr; Page 31 Elizabeth Whiting Assocs (David Lloyd); Page 32 Robert Harding Picture Library (Polly Wreford/Homes and Gardens) b; Page 34 Interior Archive (Schulenburg); Page 35 Elizabeth Whiting Assocs (John Paul); Page 37 Elizabeth Whiting Assocs (Nadia McKenzie) bl; Page 46 Paul Bricknell © BBC; Page 47 Paul Bricknell © BBC; Page 51 Robert Harding Picture Library (Simon Upton/Options) tr; Page 53 Elizabeth Whiting Assocs (Ann Kelley) tr; Page 55 Elizabeth Whiting Assocs (Tom Leighton); Page 63 Elizabeth Whiting Assocs (Michael Dunne) bl; Page 68 Elizabeth Whiting Assocs (John Paul); Page 72 Elizabeth Whiting Assocs (Jerry Tubby) t; Page 73 Elizabeth Whiting Assocs (Dennis Stone) t; McCord Design b; Page 93 Ikea.

All other photography by Mark Gatehouse © BBC.

Acknowledgements

Big, big thank yous to Ian Denning, Gemma Jackson, John and Sarah Parry and Betsy Sands for being brave enough to let me photograph in their homes – it was fun. I hope you like the results! The photos are thanks to Mark Gatehouse – his wit and energy kept everyone going.

To Guy Tortora for being a master craftsman – it is such a pleasure to see his work. To Giles Leaman for his passion and ingenuity with new or reclaimed wood. To Nishma Chandé for her talent in using fabulous fabrics and use of space. To Kay McGlone for her styling, Claire Davies for illustrations, Daisy Goodwin for the chance, Nicky Copeland and Jane Parsons for listening, Simone for keeping me going and organizing my storage, and most of all to Judy Spours, my editor, and the wonderful Oliver for keeping Reddy and Finn happy, while we worked. Judy – may we work together on many more books! You're brilliant. And, of course, to Peter, for his unending support and energy in everything I do – even storage!

Index

A album shelving, 38-9

B basement storage, 84-9
baskets:
  for vegetables, 58
  see-through, 64
bathroom storage, 66-75
battens, fixing, 39
beds, spaces beneath, 10, 22-3
bookcases, 16
books:
  and magazines, storing, 36
  arranging, 36
boxes:
  for storage, 22-3
  labelled, 30
  plastic, 81
  see-through, lightweight, 22-3
built-in systems, 14-15
  vs free-standing, 9
bunk-bed, 81

C castle toy cupboard, 82-3
catches, magnetic, 19
CD storage, 37
chest of drawers, in shed, 92
children's clothes, storage for, 24-5
children's storage, 76-83
clothes storage, 12-25
clutter:
  dealing with, 8
  storing, 26-39
  throwing out, 9
coathangers:
  hanging, 13
  matching, 23
collectables, displaying, 26-39
corner cabinet, 9
corridor, bookcase in, 36
Corshen, Sandee, 21
crafts cupboard, 78-79
cube shelving, making, 49
cupboards:
  bathroom, 67
  castle toy, 82-3
  crafts, 78-79
  doors, hanging, 19

floor-to-ceiling, 29
free-standing, 24
glass fronted, 53
hidden, 36
overhead, 17, 29
recessed, 19
sectioned, 25
shallow, 57
curtained wardrobe, 20
curtains, to hide clothes, 16, 17

D desk, customizing, 50-1
desks, 41, 42, 43, 46-7, 48, 50-1
  built-in, 42
  versatile, 50-1
desk-top, shaped, 46
displays, grouping, 30
doors, fabric-lined, 65
drawers, hidden, 27
dresser, home-made, 10, 60-1
dressing room, walk-in, 15
drying horses, collapsible, 72, 73

F fabric throw, 30-1
filing cabinets, secondhand, 42, 45-6
fireplace, as storage, 16-19, 31
floor-to-ceiling storage, 16-18
food and drink storage, 52-65
free-standing pantry, 63-4
fruit boxes, as storage, 51

G garden shed, 90-3

H hallways, 34-5
hanging cubes, 13
hanging glass shelves, 75
height, visually enhancing, 16
high-rise living, 81
home office, 8

K kitchen pan rail, 58-9
kitchen spaces, small, 54-5
knife rack, 57

L laundry, 66-73
  baskets, 72, 73

O office studies, 40-51

P pan rail, 58-9
pantry, free-standing, 63-4
pegboard, 89
potting bench, collapsible, 91
pulley system, 70-71

R recessed cupboard, 19
recycling, 60-2
Roman blind, 16, 17

S seat, built-in corner, 81
sheds:
  keeping order, 90
  two-storey, 92
shelves:
  cube, 48
  cube, making 49
  customized, 42, 45
  fixing to wall, 33
  floor-to-ceiling, 36
  for albums, 38-9
  multicoloured, 32
  narrow, 54
  open, 63
  recycled wooden, 33
  shallow, 57, 67
  shaped, 32
  stepped, 53
  shelving units, in shed, 92-3
shelving, bracket, 33
shelving, hanging glass, 75
ship-shape pulley system, 70-1
sound systems, 37
spare room study, 46-7
stairs, making most of, 27
stairway, lighting, 34-5
stairwells, 34-5

T toy cupboard, castle, 82-3

W wine rack, 63
wood, recycled, 88
workbench, 89